PEARL FISHERS

and

WANDERING GIRLS

OF LIGHT

BOOKS BY COY WILLIAMS

A Thousand Windows
Pearl Fishers
and
Wandering Girls of Light

PEARL FISHERS

and

WANDERING GIRLS

OF LIGHT

POEMS by

COY WILLIAMS

Pearl Fishers and Wandering Girls of light
Coy Williams / Napa, California
www.CoyWilliamsPoetry.com

Printed in the United States of America.

ISBN: 978-0-615-58769-1

Library of Congress Control Number: 2012907420

POETICUS®
PUBLISHING
www.PoeticusPublishing.com

For
God and Mom

CONTENTS

TRIBUTE

Search

Silence is expansive,
it reaches where the winter sun
and lonely heart sheds.

It comes to me,
with eyes that see beyond the dark.
It speaks with a soft foil
murmuring dust off petals of night.

Footsteps gentle mist
walks on the mouth of streets.
It turns the road like a desert
opening inward;
towers purple over the heart.

And I kneel with clasped hands
before the span.
Cut slits in the dark
for a holy face.

Island bound cities
float with white shadows
and speak from windows of doves,
that fly to earth's deep belly
to rest within the walls
of an all caring heart.

Morning

Waking,
her long hair
lifts half-hearted shadows
over the fields.

The light flickers in her eyes,
her cheeks blush the morning
that steps over stones
in white camellia.

Cautious,
her enormous heart
spreads out clouds like leaves,
looking for her lover.

Eloquent the whisper
lifting slowly,
her light searches the faces
in windows and doorways.

Sweet, invisible presence
once again
imagining herself.

All That Glitters

In early August
a golden glow caught my eye,
hovering shoulder high along a path.

A swirl of gnats in the evening sun
held together,
in a spinning universe all their own.

A golden fleece suspended,
for an ancient god's desire.

Their one day of life, radiant,
equal to the most beautiful
eternal flame.

These are the images
only the most ardent keep,

as we, ourselves
must fall—too soon.

Half a life

The land lives
half a life.

Beginning again
every morning,
staggering on green legs.

Born again rivers,
stretching shores
and yawning seas.

Off the pier,
children fish for Cunners
to throw to sea gulls.

Driftwood from ancient creatures
haunt the white sand,
refusing to leave.

Sea Myrtle blooms
on sand dunes,
like snow and fog rings
lifting into the azure.

Summer feeds us rainbows
behind thunder and vanilla clouds—
We mix the batter
each wanting a taste.

We eat the dream
with high summer dares—
absolute treasures
of summer love with pearls,
disguised with the sun.

Every year
we come to the shore.
We search the possible,
under the sun.

Old fishermen
who search the sea—
searched all their lives
in the sun.

Time eludes,
it ticks in the flaps of waves—
An invisible thief,
stealing the body
and leaving the heart.

And when night shades
are pulled,
and only dreams are left
to pilot their free will
across the night;

They search with the stars
for the rose on the girl's cheek
that blossomed in spring
from a fire burning sky,
bleeding on the edge of heaven.

Silence

Red sky
the delicate knife,
cuts away the evening linen.
Pink ribbons flag slowly
over the hilltop.

I live among stones
that speak smooth silence,
not of water
but without.

A long silence
before the earth shed
and the sky wept.

I speak often of silence,
it is the loudest voice.

I run along its banks,
it flows deep.
I sleep in its darkness
and I am lost.

I am the door
when no-one is there.
It knocks pleading
and I let it in.

It is your voice
between desire and presence;
absent ringing bell.

Violets and snow
scream delicate for life.
And I only know the hands,
the gentle hands that speak

of nothing and everything.

Hearts of Water

Sometimes,
in this deep falling,
I think of you.

You are the river song
singing lovers invisible,
consuming and drowning,
traveling through each other.

From the red rocks singing
dried orchards of stone
where hiding, red lions vanished
and desert gorges lay bleeding earth.

Hand in hand the memories from each pool clears,
a thought of you, a shadow darting from the rocks.

Hearts of water rushing to fill,
the bells turning
to gold.

Before Time

Before time,
when the suns of galaxies
were threads of light
woven into your hair;

My fingers
of the night sky,
would softly feel for you,
in the grass and naked trees,
flying over the sea and breadth of rivers.

In the fragrant universe of night
within the silent pulse of stars,
where the shadows and soul
merge silver on your body,
flowing music like warm rain.

My fingers move up your leg
pulling stars across your skin.

And you squeeze my hand tight
and the small, silky curve of a fallen leaf
trembles without eyes,
leaving shadows of butterflies
in silver dust,
turning in the sky.

Leap of faith

Stone made flesh,
beating without form
the song to be set free.

May I lie on my back
beneath your sister stars?
Coil in the face of you.

Let life leak out
upon the ground.
Cover it in roses.

It flows from the vise-like womb.
Screams shapeless maps
across time and love.

In every breath barely whispering
the feathered soul lifts half hearted
over echoes.

Slender hills passion,
streams the reefed corrals hand
across sunset, burning.

I cover your fields
vast and silent desire
speaking water over death.

And in the night's mouth
the air bleeds a warm sleeping breath
around the moon.

Passion burning time slows the wheel—
I leap my last breath
tattered and lonely for the light.

Above

Forgive me for remembering,
a child often needs to feel
what it was like to hold miracles
in his hands.

I hold on now for the sun,
around me the smell of dreams
and roses decay.

Over dark waters,
I hold on to my soul like smoke
lingering from ancient candles.

Deep in my chest
birds migrate crying
for the last summer's breath
when I loved you,

when in the night
a necklace of stars
fell from your neck
and I wished I could fly
above the rain and currents,

and never feel the cold air
without you.

The Loon

The voice of the loon is in me.
It feathers within my bed
all memory of you.

Ancient love calling,
spirit of the night,
who will return your call?

Has night forgotten you?
Will day sweep the voices clear
and fold its wings around you?

Will the chanting shore die
without your silver ribbons
torn in the night sky?

Will I always remember,
when your shrouded call
opened the blackness,
searching the night at the same spot,
the same darkness of this earth
alone?

Can I taste the notes in your mouth?
Can I ever live without its call?

Longing For Spring

Above the moon
lifting over ground the smell of night.

Where tigers walk on clouds
above the rain soaked gardens
in earth's upper sky.

Waltzing across the breath,
bodies of women
wrapped tight around me
and slept there.

Below, the antique lace veil,
lifts across the music
of wind and glass.

The water shines in the dark.
I hunger for your mouth
with the same desire,
divided by rain and night—
currents across the earth.

I plan to find you
in the garden dirt
if not in the water or the rose,
I will look in the air for your body
or the stars filled with light.

It Always Happens

Every time you leave me,
there is an absence I cannot explain.
Like the wind stopping on an open sea,
or hearing your voice in the other room,
long after you have gone.

It speaks from the silent leaves of roses.
It soars in the clouds overhead.
It is elusive,
like water over stones.

Like a child I turn
from your arms,
to the flutter of daybreak
as your kiss leaves the morning
without a trace.

I am jealous at life!
Taking you,
even for a moment.

And I laugh at my desire
and foolish heart to think,
the ruffled sheets on the alter you left me,
could keep me safe
from loving you.

Wandering Girls of Light

A warm breeze blows
in the summer's night.

Star skies of virgins call,
wandering girls of light.

Lanterns sway down secret passageways,
hide-a-ways in hay lofts;
beach paths in the sand,
summer fields with tall grass.

A whip-poor-will calls;
awakens the lovers of pretended deer,
of lonely innocence, of imagined playmates.

A star shoots under the wing of a tree.
Girls pretend skies
and ancient knights in stone.

Eyelids of clouds move past
propelled to sleeping—

Swirls of lanterns smoke,
dreaming in arms, magnificent.

Pray That Your Eyelids Are Flowers

Pray that your eyelids are flowers.
Pray that you believe,
wandering in the rain
for traces of warm.

But like love
lost to the night,
its blackened hair, eludes.

Blackened hair
of sea and salt
shudders so.

Cannot sleep
beneath the stars
contented flicker.

The black figure stares
from the foot of the bed;
master of the dark.

In the morning
I will burn that dark,
from the lips of a hundred lovers;
gather its ugly silence
and make bread of its tears.

Covered Their Eyes

Cliffs of green marble
covered their eyes
from the morning light.

White sand turned away
from the waves
that ran up their backs,
laid a kiss of foam
on the cheek,
before falling into themselves.

Islands don't care—
have seen enough of promises,
up to its neck with gaining
and receding tides;

tempting coins, shining beneath the waves,
ribbon waters ginger touch,
or pounding hearts with maybe's.

All love comes here,
to this shore, or that.
All looking with swollen hearts;

hoping stars, kissing stars
and dark confessions of their dreams—
and a lover saying,
it's all right.

Rain

Laughing bells
ring out your voice from heaven.
Cut loose from your full, gray fields.
Roll to the last strand of thunder,
your dark eyed desire.
Shake your head and let it fall.

Your beauty is water;
the language of the river's wide snake,
subtle black eel of the brook,
the pond's belly cupped mirror
and the seas' vast, naked back.

You sing through the babble
and clatter of the rocks,
and tease in the lifting waves
where the doves curl in foam at your mouth,
then disappear.

I am the earth you arouse.
You rub against me soft tickling
and I respond,
stirring life, milky stream pale.

And the petals of my soul break free
quivering skyward in the sun
for your cheek.

And I laugh clear my freedom over earth,
clear blue of sky and breath
in the dominion of your lips.

July

Across the summer's night,
the moon's longing
crept about in the darkness,
animal and heart.

Awakened
from the iris of the land,
the sea heated
out of a fragile glass,
breathed deeply
for a taste of air.

Even balanced,
surprised in the opening of her eyes,
the day leapt up warm out of her thighs.

Long-legged sky was waiting
and his loin was a hunting flame
and her heart without borders
loved it all.

Starlight

When evening falls to the shadows,
I travel the dark side of the world.

The cusp of the womb is starlight,
It is you.
Moon or dark faced earth,
It is all you.

As I sleep with the night,
your skin is the darkness I touch.

Reaching out to you,
there are wings in the bones of my hands
that fly to the heaven of your lips.

I love you as the star that is never seen,
a beacon that I know is there
hidden in the dark.

Old Mountain

Webbing the shoreline in Braille,
from corridors of shells
the sea keeps locked in sleep.

In oceans dark,
where salted beards of old men
breathe in skirts of jellyfish
heading for the shore.

The planets,
between lands with mouths of black rivers
that journey towards nowhere.

Red mud of the moon,
colors a sound in ripples
from rider-less clouds,

as white streets
straying from home,
look down and laugh;

along pine corridors
on a sterile mountain
without a touch,
of hot fingers tickling,
volcanic mistress, old and white.

Daylight

The moon rose triumphant,
a blind, brilliant ghost
whispering of centuries.

Ribbons wrap the seeds
of white cities in the sky.
And the crown the fog has made you,
crazy premonition over the heart,
lifts and falls
passing to the south.

The moonlight streaks the yard,
the beasts stand still.

The trees call to the shore
as the night goes out with the tide
and the waves fall into the sea.

The wind touches your face,
late and long as your lover sleeps
and signals the hour before it comes;
to hold the door
the discerning eyes,
before the fearless child, awakes.

The Conch

Breathless fog would come,
slicing the still invisible.
And a far off fog horn
will remind me,
of the waves of winter lions.

Heart in his neck,
the old horn could speak.
Beautiful, the old conch,
edges worn smooth,
black body that smelled of dirt.

The sound would echo in the woods,
past the cliffs and Crocker farm,
the Griswold's and Wyatt's field.

It was a family sound,
a signature of sorts,
that someone was in the woods.

It is my childish desire,
that we all return as before.
Before life reshaped us,
hardened us
or took us.

When one voice was clear in its direction,
that old conch
leading us home.

Black Leaves

From old men,
black leaves of the sea
turn deep in their pockets.

And the summer bones
that washed ashore,
free of purpose, now shine
and sing brightly in the sun.

In the summer of her love,
the days passed with the tide
of laughing young men,
berries never picked,
flowers and pretended kisses.

The blood of autumn harbor,
the rose curl of amber leaves,
her secret love stares constant, dying.

Into the sea
where the guitar of leaves played,
her first honest desire,

heaven and green leaves
awoke, sparkling water
in her eyes.

Stick-legged seabirds danced,
caught the curve of her breast like a wave,
scurried back and forth to the sea.

Summer Fountain

There are fields in the sky
where women's eyes are summer,
and light blue water
fingers the clouds to shape.

I search the cheek
on the hills,
and run the shadows of brooks
through the woods.

I feel on my skin
the cool petals of your breath
that lift and fall from your sparkling eyes.

And I whisper in the flow
of your hair
for your smile and lips,
to drown me.

Asking for More

The white clouds are born
in a hungry dance,
arms outstretched, spinning
against blue shoulders.

It is never tiring this game
day or night,
in a world of dark and light
only a bird can know—
That is what I want
to belong to;

in the free air, with wings
watching the moonlight
on the floor scatter,
darting flashes
over stones and sand dunes,
summer fields of hay
and glittering snow dresses of ice.

The truth, lying in the grass,
seeing through translucent screens
and oak-leaf faces.

Light, cracking open dark clouds
with thunder and lightning,
wearing sun on the arms
of shapeless giants.

Opening the eye of the land;
things of candles,
rainbows under glass with wings,
coddling a flame.

Under the arches
the eye sleeps;
figures in sand
move golden traces
into the dark light of dreams,
where vespers eyes are prayers
and the moon stares back.

Flowers we were ourselves,
searching for light
in the peak of night.
Bed and beast of gardens,
beautiful eyes in the heat of summer.

Forever falling from roses
this emery of soft divine;
its fingers holding yours,
the blue bells ringing;

it wakes the armored sea,
and calls before the light.

Opening clouds from the window
move with splendor days,
tilt warm wind without body
coming in.

Attracting afternoon hills of fire,
weaving trains of lilac
over pillars of white sky.

Fantasy in summer stars,
brighter in the beginning;
torches of fireflies
captured in jars.

I have a plea for just believing;
having known solitude,
missing something
silent and warm over me

and a voice ever
asking for more.

Resurrection

In the storm
the woods are calling
imposing questions, this gray faith.

The rain rolls in like smoke
speaking in drops
off the shelves of leaves
to the forest floor in whispers,
with a thousand lips calling me to rest.

Walking upon the damp humus
I hear a voice through the windows of rain.
Come! These hands will sooth you,
throw back your head and drink from my mouth.

Turn inward!
There is no sun to guide you now,
only the path of your heart.

Together you can cry unnoticed
with the weeping fog;
the footsteps of your worry will disappear
into the soft sod.
Come! Together we will hide the pain
under the leaves and rocks;
in the fire of the earth.

Let's bow our heads beneath the branches.
Together, we will sing through the storm,
in luminous voice, up through the tiers spiral.
Through the corridors and torrents you can weep,
until the weeping stops for the voice that sleeps,
in the morning light.

Spring Song

From winter
I listen for your voice
in the silent moon.

I try not to remember
the flower of your passion,
the feel of your body
haunting me over smooth shoulders of fog,
your soft breath pulling me in the night.

I breathe trembling water,
a thousand sparrows flickering
in my lips.

Hovering over your fields,
the wings beat in my chest
gurgling the racing waters
down brooks of melting snow.

Up from your damp sod,
your sea continues to swell
as your hair of sunlight
sweeps across my chest.

Sweet spring of desire,
calling my name
beneath the earth.

April

Rain and sun become music.

A Red-winged blackbird,
bobs on a blade of grass.

An eagle lifts a fish from the lake,
effortlessly.

And the grunions come home
with the tide.

And in the night's mouth,
the air leaves a warm, sleeping breath
around a yellow moon.

In the black pond's reflection,
peep frogs shout their desire.

Spring rain has thrown its nets,
earth inspires for tomorrow's cities
of green and crimson.

Time returns,
into the body of another.

Like a bird flying through smoke,
and the sea falling into itself.

Locket

Enclose me;
though I have closed myself
from the fingers of the day.

I want to hear your voice
shatter the glass of my heart,
the way water speaks
to the rocky shore.

The way rain dreams of home
and red wakes the sky.

I want defiant words
pushing me open to hear
your love
demanding mine;

and whispers,
for that stolen moment
of home.

Resonance

It has been so long
since I heard your voice.

When I sleep,
faces and bodies
pass through layered thoughts of consciousness,
disappearing without color.

Life's insipid prose
has caught me like a river,
pulling me in a day to day
without sound.
Vacant rooms without light or darkness.

The longings are not the same.
My thoughts are one mixed sea of poetry.

I go to bed hungry
to hear your arms.

Cedar Chest

All your memories were kept,
in the sweet smelling cedar chest.
Dried red roses with brittle stems,
faces on photographs, consumed by time.

You smiled, then tears.
As a child I asked, what's the matter?
In silence you held something,
and in that silence, I became scared.

As if the weight of dreaming has taken you
and the mercy of the world,
within the tapestry you held,
could somehow take you away from me.

All your jewelry packed away,
with everyday secrets
that no one will ever know.

A light in your hands became brilliant,
to the point I could no longer see you.

I woke up
and was alone;
pretending my life,
fooling myself with happiness.

I went outside to write my name in the earth
and water it, until the bells stopped ringing.

Little Black Tears

Old horsemen swirl in the great hall
where you danced long ago,
and I remember your eyes
staring at me across the night.

But you loved him like the earth,
where you grew in his shadow
and hoped when the time was right
the sun would return you
to his great arms
named forever.

Now you're the moon,
hiding in the day;

your heart lifts skyward
like clouds of blackbirds
changing form,
circling with a thousand eyes
opening and closing;

your body of secrets,
blankets the night—

Pretending not to wake you,
the horsemen weave through
the constellations;

the stars fall
splintering from heaven,
little black tears.

Night Books

In a paragraph of her lips,
the words are seeds
open to fly,
tasting each other
like dirt and rain.

The salt is a naked shadow
of a woman's deep and endless desire,
holy water to bathe his face.

And the mask that he wears
is only leaves falling,
and the thief of the moon is a poem,
pages of white echoes
from the heart,
that lift and turn to doves
in her hands.

Candle Smoke

I remember when you came into my life.
Barely a whisper, wind at the door.
Across the room gliding with ease,
a swallow carrying ribbons of light.

And I wanted you
in that moment, like a flower.
To hold beauty,
to claim for myself, your sweetness.

I never imagined out of such a look
my desire would grow.
To what end, my love would go weeping
in the harvest of your heart.
And in your arms
the language would be molded,
flamed in passion.

We were one form,
a wick muddled fate,
burning itself without end.

And the spirit in which we burned
lit the night beyond all words,
the air filled
eternity.

Glass Lightly

In the fall
I will find you,
through doors in dark hours,
on amber stems behind the tears,
in fading ghosts of light.

Curling the sunset plains,
shadows running across the fields,
whip back from the wind.

Ghosts rise, to stroke the cat's back,
lifting within the trees moonlight,
lay their flame, dying in water.

Circular man of string
wraps the leaves with wind,
tosses promises, crackling in flames.

Dancers leap in petals,
pulled up from the ocean floor,
as sea shells rise
in the whale's rainbow.

Moth

When the weight of dreaming
has taken you—
Two lovers
hold the golden lamp.

Opening through the darkness
a white moth dreams
mysterious circles,
and the spinning light
becomes bodies, opening and closing.

From flesh to wind
the flame is emerald,
and the tiny eyes tremble
closing once, twice,
then flashes to smoke.

Two Hearts

Away from you,
the day has two hearts.
One with desire of your mouth and body
which beats with fire,
the other beats softer, coming sweet,
like a child's love wrapped around my neck.

Images of your body flash through the day
over streets and objects without form,
appearing like swallows darting past.
And my blood is hot from it,
and it takes over like rain.

Then softly,
the tears of your life come to view,
like snow and music
and I am helpless but to love you.

And I hold you as an ancient love
both father and mother and words.
All in one desire to reach the pain,
to stroke your hair
until your heart runs clear
with room to love me.

To fall together in that grasp
of spirit and sky.
Where our bodies take over
both animal and breath.

And when we meet later on our
words are but shields
from the thoughts of the day,
looking for the door to open
the sky again.

Vespers

Woman of my thirst—
infinite longing.

The night holds you in a sign
burning for me,
ancient symbols of a prayer.

Scattered eyes pull me in,
one to the next.
Petals flickering
a thousand breaths.

I am yours, listening for voices
over riverbeds
crying water on a distant moon.

From this garden hungry to know you,
to make some connection,
your mouth opens between points on a map
that speak beyond the dark expanse
of lovers arching in the nights blackness.

My Mother, in Heaven

You left behind
Silver petals of ashes,
and a memory of your smile.

I can feel you,
your love is the stillness
the absence of everything,
the living of everything.

I know my words cannot be answered
but I feel an answer in the stars.
I know you are part of all that now
and again, all of nothing.

The open door that you traveled through
has closed behind you
and the brightness of its virtue,
only a vague shadow.

The elegance of the blue road
is clouded white with miles of prayers,
dipping and gathering into birds.

I know the answers
but find myself questioning everything
as if I was new to eternity,
bathed as a child singing in white temples,
the secret of being alone.

Picture Albums

Filtered light through Venetian blinds
bleeding through my fingers,
cutting the lines of my face,
a face forever passing through mirrors.

Pushing up these windows
glassless into the edge of the sky,
the sunlight flames the clouds
caught between doors of empty hallways.

I step down carpet-worn stairs
along silent, poorly lit corridors
to daylight and park bench wastelands.
From worn pockets, holding my dreams out
one by one, to pigeons
that fly away.

Returning to rented hours;
hands washed in years of weathered rain,
rest themselves
in armchairs and pale white stares.

Behind doors with teacup sighs and broken voices
in afternoon plays,
there, left breathing to the tick, of the clock
in white robes peeking out from behind the shades.

I can't turn away the stranger's face,
out windows, fading mirrors and absent looks,
from the tired worn beds unmade,
the foolish smiling child
sitting captive to dreams, escapeless,
in the afternoon of picture albums.

Dream After

Twilight earth,
your heartbeats
crosscurrents.

Your love is a dream
sang aloud
with the rain.

Elephants gather
beneath the trees.
Leaves turn sun
into shade.

Open plains on a sea
born green, then gold,
sleep in the blazing
afternoon.

Turning over,
the universe comes back
after counting diamonds
on its belly.

Starved for more bleached bones,
night cries at water holes,
raise heartbeats
for a kingdom served.

Animals sleep standing,
leaning against acacias
listening,

for the dream after.

The Last Garden

Mournful sweet,
delicate petals fall
burning on the water.

Traveling to the ground,
oceans of leaves
breathe in forest's waves
pursuing each other;

Swirling in the sun,
expanding to flowers,
the spiral lanterns
among the clouds
fly for the unimagined
darkness.

Their hearts now guard the walk
once strewn with flowers
of insatiable lust,

as butterflies search
in tears for honey;

Above a chorus,
trembling with birds.

Night Candles

Nightly under the simple stars
blessed among birds
flickering twilight of souls.

A soft bell curled, blessed
of wounds and white talc.

Island of warm tears
down white thighs;

stiff sand of milk,
throwing bones
into the darkness.

The red blood
dries in the flames
along beaches' white secrets.

Candlelight in your hair
makes men pray
in the damp love darkness.

Heroes forgotten for a moment
in drowning seas
of loves house.

Untitled

And I wished to die,
not knowing you would leave me—

And the sons and daughters of the leaves,
would fall in autumn
and the blood between words and life
would go on,
past the winter fear
reaching a pure absolute place,
swirling strips of gold
that never touch the ground.

A Mysterious Man

A mysterious man
has rainbows
in his mouth.

Knowing he can't stay,
she loves him
when he leaves,
carrying his shoes
filled with stars.

It is a long dream he carries,
and he sleeps with coins
in his eyes
and splintered mirrors
of the sky.

Always searching for
a bell with green eyes.

And lanterns carried by gypsies,
and virgins who dance
in the glow
of the north star.

And he loves to sing
with their early skies.

White dresses
make dreams
in the clouds;

and his hands
a teasing smile
of rain.

When Leaving the Shore

I will live in the woods,
where the leaf's edge is blue
and the dream twilight opens.

From the dark dirt
the light ripples on the sea
and the waves cry.
Opening flower, the blood turns black
then gold.

I will whisper to you
from the clouds
if you cannot already see,
the roses behind me
and the birds at my feet.

Butterflies

Two butterflies
spinning as one.

White petals
playing with the wind.

Again and again
into each other;
a warm breath
of music.

Hitting the water,
the music stops.

A sail on the horizon—

White butterfly
at the waters edge—
a flickering movie shutter
making a path
for the moon.

Because Of You

Pressed against me
arms connected,
your soft burning voice
is an endless river that glistens,
on golden river streams,
on thoughts washed and tumbled.

I love you
as my heart opens and closes,
empties and fills.

I have peered out this window before
on life's changing face.
Eyes in a photograph I can't recall.
Untouchable secrets as a boy
in beautiful, lazy summers.

I close the curtain
as sunlight feeds the small man
standing near the fence.
And he is staring up at me as a red rose.
And I am veiled with planets spinning,
my breath born in a blinding light.

Only God can see through me
singing the years invisible,
before I knew life,
before I would come to life,
because of you.

Summer Leaves

In the green
of summer leaves,
I see transparent faces.

Branches with arteries of armies
growing one behind the other,
fingers becoming walls
of green barriers.

I pretend the innocence
that I feel for them,
pretend unafraid
that the autumn to come
will not take them.

And the shade that is my life,
beneath a darting palladium
flickering coins of light,
I hide dressed in oak, dirt and stone.

I will sound the colors
before them,
to atone for their death,
and weep though I know not why.

Fall

Out of the blossoming wake,
in love and sympathy made her own,
the dream tide eddies.

Time was her labyrinth
in which she was entirely lost,
entirely bound for his kiss.

Her heart, loose at one end
was a mystery to her,
an enchanted swirl
hundreds of leagues deep

whipped the shore ringing underfoot
like plates of glass,
and in the center of that vast, silent sea
the name of this languid stillness
was his arms.

Poetic voice of autumn,
voice of the wind cut leaves
rustling in her lips.

October

October night,
hallow moon.

Black fingers in open sky
grabs the darkness across the mouth
burning voice of leaves.

Great river among the branches
rattle the swords awake.

Trees bow with lowered heads
and face the ancient wound—

Stare the giants hooded face
into the autumn wind,

cry roses heart of gold
as winter lifts its hand

and calls the girl across the field
to kiss her lips with snow.

Deer Hunter

When I was young in winter
in the woods of my home,
sleeping apples called out to the deer
and the sun would sound the warm opus,
rising cords of smoke.

Hunters of the fields,
my brother and I
searched for the deer
in haphazard wanderings,
following tracks through the woods,
and searched in the moonlight
for his face.

Apollo brother do you hear me?
I have blown the horn, calling you in the woods.
I have searched for you in the cedar grove
and in the rain for your voice.

Gone now with the silver body of snow,
bleeding water high above the ridge
where you went to wear the mask of the deer
and antlers my brother.

And in the alder swamps
and on the rubbing tree
you left your mark for me.

And I will remember
your tracks in the snow
and how I loved you
before I knew what love was.

My dear, ominous soul,
I will never forget
as I take your memory whole,
over my shoulders
through the alders
and out the blizzard's mouth.

November

November left blind
splendor in her voice,
calling out the frost
blankets of diamonds, speechless.

Hanging crystal branches
chimes broken bones,
over the white earth, eyes gleaming.

In the sun
she cries the tears
that are not her own,
belonging to the child not yet born
beneath the earth singing.

In the air
the sweet, ageless tide,
of fallen maples
and rotting oaks,
drifting in and out, over the snow.

Her face is of whispers that speak of death
from the cold silence of the deer,
in the deep woods there.

She enters through the doorway at dusk
and the heavy sky that she wears,
falls away to smoke.

At the hearth
I feel the embers of her eyes,
as a spring of flames
crackle across my heart.

The Key

I put your body
on the face of smooth stones,
and those stones on the face of stars.
I rub the day below the belly
as my footsteps fill with ashes.

The absence is deafening still.
A wounded animal cries
between thoughts
and silence.

A symphony plays,
harbors the slate gray lock,
its rusted face weeping.

When I was with you,
both innocence and fire
burned the fields red.
Now from this door,
the night holds its hand
over my eyes.

Alone,
in a turn, beneath this heart,
the vast plain opens
where we hid as children
within the grass,
stealing passion,
dreaming the sky of clouds.

I was only a dream.
And you were only poetry.

Baptismal

Mother of the sea
I cry for you.
Haunting me, your rhythmic breath
calls me back.

Your sacrament of white foam
pulled by the tide,
comes miles to the shore
to feel the bones of my feet.

Shifting sand races underfoot,
swirling fingers
curl into anklets of seaweed.
Wind gusts like trains in my ears.

Lift me! Flay my open heart!
Whip my body naked, senseless with air!
Cut me to flesh and bone.

Submerged in your blood,
purify me in the salt of your womb;
dissolved to blindness,
unearth me to spirit.

Use one cry to call me back,
I will find the light.
Up the white stem
forming current,
bursting forth.

I will hold my breath
between your legs.
Through the rain soaked forest
we will burn the new song together,
the music of birth.

Single Thread

I am alone
so my writing lacks a voice
from the other room.

Lacks a meal,
for the hungry.

I write only about bits and pieces
of love's memory.

No warm shadow to follow me
or hand to cool my fever.

It is poetry alone as my love.
Poetry, that made up my wild heart.

Its desire imagines.
Its longing imagines the most of beauty
and the frailty of small things.

I am the owner of the sunlight;
of my own darkness.

My childhood of scattered leaves
brings me peace—
toward the evening writing,
towards currents felt, unseen.

It is what I do.
No way to explain it.

I make it rain,
I make the sun dry every leaf,
every hand;

And if there is nothing more,
I will lift a fog bow into the
sky and give it reason.

My truth relies on your memories,
your life strings hidden, un-played.

One word can free you— as love,
as death—destroy you,
or make you search for the meaning
I never intended.

Cut me!
Feed a raven my tongue.
Open my love, or wound me,
judge me, or scowl.

Honey me, hate me
but go on reading.

Dam my beauty— my only thing
I can give you!

A tower to be higher on;
a hope to be stronger,
and a voice
I could never give you.

Earthworks

There are voices rotting
leaves with timeless care;
seasoned stacked,
murmuring dark purpose.

Inside you where the sound is deafening,
deep decay falls off burning silence.
My hungry root penetrates your moist sod.
The fingers go deep,
careful not to disturb your winter's late friend.

Below the skin our tapestry blooms.
I take your essence without a word;
Clutching white stones and amber,
you lean back.
Our bodies soaked
in corridors of laughter,
white stems reaching the touch.

Hungry mouth open,
the dark planet sifts through the last storm.
The spine heaves the roof's canopy
calling currents, running deep.

Holding on to one another
we curl beneath the long white pitch.
Gripping the rail
our fingers hold tight to the ice,
the snow's white breath to break,
feeling blind
for the coast of spring.

Sweet One

Cobblestone England, the Lord's descent.
Foot-locker journey
long to the place,
where the sunrise on the morning mast
and the orange glow,
touches on everything America.

I remember when dishes in the hutch
had shown the finest china
and the Irish filled the cups of guests,
and the red rose that she wore
hooked deep its thorn in cameo white aster
against a blue sky.

I remember the harbor
in her frenzied midday spell,
where black sweat and burlap
mixed with the smell of the sea,
and the moving sky rolled with the waves,
as captured faces searched the docks
with motherless eyes,
entranced, conclusion
in cane-sweet America, with ebony seeds.

And from the swelling calm and patient earth,
the cornucopia autumned
and the Indian summer
sweetly sang from her fields.

And the grapes that grew from the Promised Land,
clustered warm on the vine.
Through insipid summer
their passion grew,
bleeding joy for burning lips,
toast the wedding and sang.
Engaged the land, the dream together
yellow mustard, golden ring.

Within the iris, the rose, the grape's red heart,
into the song it all goes.
Into the seeds and voice, wilderness and desire,
into the singing blood.
Where the eyes cannot see
and dreams cannot yet vision, it all goes.
Through history's ringing steps,
into the soul's deep heart and out again.

The hand holds tight
this song of the earth,
the sweet ones, mothers bleed.
America's orb, the umbilical stem,
the child beyond the seed.

Autumn Tree

With her red
and deepening heart,
a warm pulse
moves closer,
beat by beat
in the cold.

Afraid in the longing
of distant birds
flying away—

Afraid in believing
winter will be kind,
not knowing who it was
on the other side
of her skin.

Not knowing
as before, who loved her.

On what sea to pass,
when the leaves would be green
and she can see again.

Now the beat relapses,
and a touch
pulling, deepening
and persistent;

down to the roots echo,
for her children.

Tears fall,
she blesses the earth.

Water Music

If you find me
off the Solace Major,
sitting alone
in the white bloom of stars;

I will be reaching out
in the night dream
composing;
sea shells
with whale songs,
birds in allegretto.

Feet in the water;
notes dangling from docks,
bob on staffs below.

Above the lake,
long shadows dance
with golden gowns—
swirl in speechless clouds,
staring back with an audience of birds.

Planet echoes— sweet water,
sunset taps inhale me,
into the night.

Crows of October

The waiting moon in yellow,
swims slowly to a spot—

Up the ramp of a hill,
for a silver fork of trees
to hold her side by side,
until sea legs are found
for the open sky.

This black sleep with no eyes
has a heart that burns
honey into salt.

A ghost in the moon
silhouettes the night,
in trees that move as if leaving,
but never leave;

Sway with stomachs
full of wings;

Eyes watching
with black plums.

Pearl Fishers

There are times
in this longing,
I forget how to feel.
Only silence can describe the numbness.

Along your side,
I could remember the window of your breath,
and the sand's persistence.
I try to remember your kiss with that same everlasting.

How I tasted your lips
on a wet tongue of air,
and pretended
there was nothing between us.

Love is a fog that becomes music;
A bird bobbing on a blade of grass,
its balance of weight and stillness,
the pulse and the blood
held together, singing.

And your heart that I used to know
spoke to me of oceans,
and the weight
time has on the heart.

And I breathed in for you,
and for all the fishers
that circled above.

Promises

She thought of where the mind opened out
the safe falling of the words would save her
beneath the dark invisible, a place to hide.

Feeling the sculpture of his face,
brown sand and sea milk
in a cup full of promises
across her lips—

angels struggle to be free
as the glass breaks a thousand streams
of birds.

Red Lips Postulate

Men are mirrors
for women to learn
how to see themselves.

Green diamond eyes,
smooth reaching stems.

The summer's daze
stirred his heart
with a touch.

The grass transforms the desire
to roses, to cure the ache of spring
as a universe grows stars.

The illusion,
that he lived at all without her
was his measure of fate.

She was a warm moment
that comes with the sun,
but never leaves.

It is against logic, a women's work;
their fulfillment of desire,
opening concrete with pillows,
softening a man's destiny.

Red lips postulate,
the soft will of echoes.

Rising Moon

Rising moon
of a thousand faces
and my heart an island of sand.

Nobody but you
in a moment
could stop me,
your lips of silver and dark.

The thirst always calls me
back to the night,
back into your arms
until my eyes
are full of wings.

On Wednesday

The animals were quick
and fed leisurely on my body.
My skull seemed awkward now,
larger and out of place with the rest.
The bones laughed easy,
shining, scattered like a white rosary,
broken in the leaves of grass.

This is the land I finally see,
hidden desert in the growing grass,
vision upward to the open sky,
bound and free.
Free from the darkness beneath.
Free from inheritance,
rituals and plot.
Free of lilac in the dooryard blooming
and gathering voices from vacant lots.

No veiled women's verse to soothe
or solid coffins laugh.
No pilot's hand to steer the bar
or face to face assume.
No miles to go, for woods or shore,
the autumn tide is still.
The odor of life has ended long,
the open sky has filled.

Time weaves the grass around me,
decay and tapestry.
I hold to every thread,
straining to see
where the two lines will cross
from twilight and horizon,
shroud to swaddling.

I peer out to the distant,
magnificent rib cage,
bleached like ivory gates.

Birth Light

Aboard the beasts the children ride
on clouded bridges linking the sky
to the water's edge.

In smoke their curling voices vanish
when light touches them.

Drops of amber
wakes roots, reaching hands,
pulling underground a secret sun,
giving life a shadow
to follow back upon the earth
with eyes and breath evergreen.

My love is the birth blood
of a flowered moon
and a mother's voice.

I know there is more
to the beauty of women that draws me
to starry eyes and summer dresses.

I have a thirst for fire
and a burning need to drink
from your mouth.

The forest from which I came
from the womb and desire,
up the scorched trunk through winter,
through dark channels searching
for the light of your voice.

For the birth sound that shimmers
out the branches, through the air,
in the throats of doves.

Her Dream Was the Universe

In the sand
beneath the shifting, dark mantle,
layers dream the summer's rain
stacked one by one over voice.

Once
roses epiphany
arbored the great columns' thigh,
calling into the flames.

She knew in the stars
when the dark magnificent
would leak out
upon the ground.

And in time
I would come to rub away the veil,
covering her lips.

The sun of her passion still burns
the cheek within the ashes.
Her wind moving over syllables
speak of roses
and kisses.

My hands
sift the still breath
between sand and desire,
in a land I have never been.

Beneath her body burns
a garden of tears
flooding the chamber with horses,
running ribbons around
lovers and kings.

Evergreen

Relentless is my song
that never stops.
It grows outward
as a shadow of a bird,
silent as a woman's hair
wanting to be touched.

I miss you in these days,
when the gray veil of longing
stretches on the road
with rain,
and curls the night
with waves of music,
lifting and falling.

I dream
invisible currents,
like heaven eclipsed by birds,
their song
cutting through skies' eternity,
evergreen.

Red Spider

I don't know if the red spider
on the African plain will miss it.

Or in the wide sea,
if the whale's song
will show a change.

Will the white crane sensing it,
slow its step for me?

Will the orange dawn,
feather the field
one last time?
And snowcaps weep,
as I close my eyes?

Will the girls miss me,
in the summer grass?
Gathering wild kisses
in the sun.

Will autumn blackbirds, of swirling smoke,
feeling a loss within their pattern,
suddenly close formation?
Or will they leave a place of honor,
for me?

The earth is hungry just one more time
and the maples and the birches
fill the air with voice.

I will pass through the twilight
of the poets,
their eyes gleaming like stars.

They will sniff the dirt
and grass from my body
and search my pockets for leaves
and smooth stones.

The earth is hungry just one more time
and the maples and the birches fill the air.

Tide Pools

Away from you,
life's frenzy lapped
its ivory tongue.
Moss on the temple stones,
the arch over the bed.

A song without words
feels its way on the shore,
deep sea, red soundless.

Your body is the sky,
turning over burning sand.
Your hand searches for the child
among the sea shells,
a piece of driftwood,
a small heart beating.

Broken wings in your breast
that can not fly anymore,
long for love and stars

and the wings of children.

Ancients

I see glaciers in the light
and I hear swallows
gliding over the sea of glass, radiant.

Across centuries they moved,
in lands where the dark forests grew.
Where ancient women once gathered wood
for the fire to make bread.

And this world was bread,
consistent to the taste of blood,
the salt of the earth.

And I breathe their words
lingering in the air.
And I feel a presence
from that time,
from my father's father.

I long to live within their voices,
and resound their past in the frozen smoke.
I want to hear of the deer and the forests,
the horses and the rivers they broke
sounding hooves rushing over water.

I want to sing of the Great Spirit,
whose land it was and whose body
was the seed and tongue curled stream,
passing down the roads' twilight.

Take me where the fogbow curling mist rises,
after the rain calls the sun.
Make me a necklace, proud earth,
of seeds and feathers, claws and teeth.
And give me strong arms of copper and longbow.

Speak softly from the name
carved in the white oak and hemlock,
beside the stream that still flows
in her eyes.

Speak now from the sentry
from the seasons watch,
with coat flowered woods with wings,
to the sky of warbled gray windows.

White Heron

Where does it go,
the souls' white heart;
the moon's petals
falling on black glass?

With the tide's endless pull,
oblivion floats white
bobbing and turning
music to wind.

What has brought you
to this outlet,
stalking the weeds,
icy spear, burning hot?

Yours is not the dream of water
or the stars mouth open.
It is not a flame
that draws your face
to the pool.

Your moon hovers
for more then a breath,

it stares down for me.

Bone Fish

The sun burns the blue oracle,
tracing the sky in a boundless sea.

It is endless this constant ringing bell,
melodic voice through metal
holding my body.

Between the dull curve and stone face,
I search the gardens'
sentient flowers.

The white violin weeps
and the voice heats the water
through my body.

It is the steel hook
that pulls me
as thunder sweats the cord
from silence.

The River Where She Sleeps

A river flows into infinity,
a silk train of black
on passageways,
bare shoulders high,
carries a bird with a broken wing.

Spoken words
beneath an ocean of itself,
two sisters talk of death,
then turn their eyes away.

The eyes of heaven steady,
white clouds shutter
the sun's rays across the room.

No more tomorrows?
And the truth turned away.

Across dark galaxies desert,
a twig snapped.
No! You are still young,
running in the woods.

On a path towards sunset
an old man with a white beard
pushes a cart
into the August night,
bumping stars on strings.

There is a road that travels alongside
the river where she sleeps,
crossing and re-crossing
until vanishing within.

Song of the Tide

Swirling,
her cape romantic.
Winds of white music,
spray the air with doves.

Upward pockets of cold and warm,
streak the night in northern lights,
across a galactic spine.

Between each other they nod,
to the same direction,
those herds of moving gray
that come for miles undaunted,
all blind, gentle beasts
pulled to their careless bay.

Lifting her eyes inland,
she moves deep and wanting.
Her solvent womb holds a red hunger.
Her vivacious bloom lifts the throbbing swell,
to plunge and crawl the soft sod.

She licks her teeth
within the broken rocks,
her breath low, rising to foam,
breaks the open air,
pulled deep to scrape the sandy lust,
that rolls off shoulders
of smooth stones,
against the relentless sleep.

Music Keeper

With the heart of a violin
opening the night,
I write black lines
for the green and beautiful earth.

Notes in birch bark drawn faces,
in winter air with suspended hands.

In the woods
I hear for the leaves,
and for the rain.

At dusk,
sleepy day silence closes for crickets,
loud again in the grass.

The magnificent wheel of stars
turns in ancient ascent,
over Orion's shoulder calling.

At the end of the distance
a pure whisper floats,
crested between sleep and thought,
a past lover ellipsing.

The great joy of a glass sea is waiting,
and rivers running between pillows
of golden hills sleeping.

The sunset of desire stares back
like a bodiless note suspended,
suffering out of place—
music waiting to be written

as a consortium of angels
sing in the air.

Approaching Rain

Shadow people,
hunched under arches of fog
float down hills of black.

Strands of a woman's hair
hang down sweeping the ground,
over fields and woods
with bristled backs,

over shoulders
and headlands drop,

to scattered islands,
tapping whispers on rooftops
and prayers across the glass,

weep of deserts and salt
turning to rivers,
bleeding into oceans.

The Land's Children

The land's children,
within the land and sea that covers them.

In the deep woods,
they sing of the summer fields
turning grass to hay,
and play in the musk of the brook's leaves.

They have no home;
it is their longing that is home.
Sky and trees,
are their head and arms,
with cupped hands
asking more from the rain.

Their feet pretend voices,
leaving names of gold
with histories of sunlight and path,
where waves wash them away,
beautiful children of sand.

Night Bird

I hear in the wind
low breathing calling me to the sea.

From these petals' open lips,
I soar in the night sky
on the endless mouth of surf,
crying echoes above the waves.

I cut the slits of air and voice,
flip over darting the light.
Speeding towards the moon,
running from the shadows of wolves,
on the glass below.

Effortless, these pastures,
as I dance across the dark cathedral
of night.

Raven

I ride the edge from wolves and twilight.
Dark cavern, ravenous death,
dwells the flying thief
stealing golden crumbs.

I am drawn to him,
neither master or friend,
I hold out my hand anyway.
My broken bread of dreams
I will share.

Come here!
Tell me what is behind your dark eyes
and why you hunger so,
for my last breath.
Why do you wait so calmly for me?
cutting the soft throat of day
with your cry.

Can you tell me if hell has teeth,
and heaven but temperate lips?
And might I hear angels
as I pass down your throat's
black dominion,
to silence.

Kisses from the Dead

So many nights
I spoke your name
as you slept.

Hearing you breathing
next to me,
with the sound of a cricket
outside the window.

I asked, why am I here?
The cricket answered for you.

Love asleep,
under the blue road,
on silver rivers of dust.

Beneath your eyelids
a different name
sleeps with you.

Rainbow beneath the mountain,
kisses from the dead.

Coming Home

Make me a place
beneath the field
where the grass is tall and golden.

Let me soar
when the rotting turns to air
this child of fire.

Show me the brook
where the Red-winged blackbird sings.

Lay your breath on my cheek,
one last time.
Kiss the ache from my long journey.

Your love will carry me through
the great mouth,
where the torrents and dark
become light.

Lead me across the meadows
to the seas' black glass.

Open the door
if it will not open.
Hold my hand
so I will not be afraid.

Sing the song I longed to hear,
open my eyes
so I can see.

Voices

And the dark voice
watching curls on waves
wash over naked pillows of black,
give in and break.

Softening sunlight,
pulls open the clouds;

a daughter's head
peeks out at the knees,
eyes shining.

And her light-voice reflects
in segmented sun-bleached bones
and chains of blue-green seaweed,
glittering off a shoulder of sand.

Water music plays from her hair,
in wind strands of lariats on the sea,
pulling tide pools back under the glass.

Foot prints of lost voices wander,
disappearing at the edge
from sleepy eyelids of milk.

Sirens carry sea-baskets
back to the land
dreaming of love—
humming birds
in their mouths.

Around us

Around us
soft lace of snow.
Winter's hands held high
gathering leaves,
spires of ash.

Music in the dark;
shapeless galaxies,
green eyes awake.

White fingers,
crack the cold lands
under the earth.

Heated by the sun,
melted snow bleeds into furrows,
opening eyes
of dandelion seeds

that float down the terrace walk,
tumbling;
pause unsure,
then continue.

He stumbles through them.
Her steps coming down the
walk, frees him.

God now of his bones,
she lays her reef.

February

Bring to me
the taste of your lips on the rain,
as Spring comes fragrantly with your dress,
over the reef of the moon laid out.

And on your cheek, crystal voyage innocence,
plays the child of sleep.

Beautiful white web, roses along your walk,
temple green space between the snow.

The music of your body is soft fire
and the white fog along your side,
stirs me.

And I open my heart
to the soft blending
of your words,

from a thousand wings,
in your touch.

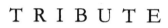

TRIBUTE

Neruda

Silent it speaks
off the shores of Isla Negra.

In the sky's ashes,
on the lips of waves
it calls out his name.

The blade of his figurehead
cuts open the sea
curling foam before him
as he rides across the dark expanse.

The silent women of death
kneel at his feet.
He knows all of them by name;
Air, Sea, and Starlight.

He has seen them before
from the summit of the cliff
through the window of the earth
walking out on the water
pointing to the country
in the burning night sky.

He must go!
The embers call him,
the ship has pulled its anchor
one last time across the breath.

And the hand beneath the waves
recedes motionless.

And the bells!
I cannot speak of the bells!
They drink from his mouth
off the shores of Isla Negra.

The waves are horses
rushing back to the trees;
the wood and the hands that carved them.

Ships in bottles break free of glass
and set sail off the window's ledge
to search for him in the dust, covered sea.
And the grieving hearts cut tributes
in the wooden palings.
Currents deep pulling voice
float high in the wind
above his house in Isla Negra.

And he feels their words
cut upon his heart
and he hears the tremble
resound the hills
in wings overhead,
as he walks in the universe
through the tears ancient mirror of twilight;
in the hands of rain
reaching,
for the earth

In Granada, on the road to Alfacar,
There stands the, Fuente Grande, The Great Fountain,
That sings for a poet.

The Great Fountain

Come dance through me
in this ancient body
aligned with the stars wheeling.

Day will fall into night
and your pain and shadows
will fill my empty glass
and I will drink your darkness
with the light.

And a thousand wings
will blush the pillars of rose
within an ocean of polar eyes.

And the blood will thunder
through the great heart
and the tiny fingers
will reach over the arctic sun
to touch the hand
dreaming of warmer birds.

Ode to the Death
of Garcia Lorca

I want to speak to you
of Garcia Lorca's last words,
that wept from the pores of every being.

The white stone bleeding red,
crying, No! Take me! Take me!
I was a worthless rock without him.

The Black Cactus in the afternoon sun,
shadowless. Take me! Take me!
I can suffer the cold of your fears,
cut me, as I have cut you. I will bleed for him.

Take me! Take me! The Sage Deer cried, eat me!
I can nourish your emptiness,
he can only nourish your soul.

Take me! Take me! Cried the scorpion,
I am your enemy underfoot.
I hold your poison scepter,
he your conscience sweet.

And the golden brook forever running said,
Take me! My song!
I will dry so moss, brittle, crumbles
and grass grows long between my teeth.
 Take me! Take me!

And the birds flying cried,
Can't you see? Can't you see? Take me! Take me!

And the moon said, it is I who is your threat,
for every face that looked up to me.
It is I you want,
for every soul that longed in the night,
I am the only beacon, I am the only light.

And love's timeless rose cried,
Take me! Take me! I will die for you,
and there will be no more roses.
Kill my love forever! Please! Please!
I beg you! Take me! Take me!